NOW

poems by

Karen Moulton

Finishing Line Press
Georgetown, Kentucky

NOW

Editor: Christen Kincaid

Cover Art: Anne Criss

Author Photo: Vivian Su

Cover Design: Elizabeth Maines

Printed in the USA on acid-free paper.
Order online: www.finishinglinepress.com
also available on amazon.com

Author inquiries and mail orders:
Finishing Line Press
P. O. Box 1626
Georgetown, Kentucky 40324
U. S. A.

Table of Contents

For James

Widow

God damn you Jack!
Why'd you have to fall down?
I tried to hold onto you,
tried like hell to fix
your broken crown.
But you left me alone,
with an empty pail,
at the bottom of the hill.

Our House in the Woods

Sitting on the back deck
I listen as birds perform
amaranthine arias, pine
needles shush upstart
maples, while inside
the refrigerator chants
its mechanical mantra. These
are the sounds that fill
my ears, these, and the loud
absence of your voice.

Selfish

I still haven't lifted the lid
of your jade urn, haven't sifted
your ashes through my fingers.
You didn't want me to do anything
with them. You didn't even want
me to keep them. How could I
grant you that? I needed to have
some part of you and even though
I haven't so much as looked
at your ashes, I feel you there
when I lay my hands on the solid
green sides of your urn that sits
beside the fireplace. I know how
much you hated the cold. Every fall,
you'd start to cocoon yourself
in blankets while I became energized,
face flush from the brisk breeze. You
didn't want to be put into the ground,
you said, couldn't abide the thought
of being buried beneath the cold earth,
hated the idea of using land for the dead.
I sit and watch the logs glow red with heat.

Living Room

This room was built from cedar, pine, and rock.
Twin skylights drape it with their strands of light,
a clutch of pinecones lends its scent. Two chairs,
the brown of Earth, the tan of sand, afloat
on silken threads of cherries and blue seas.
Awash with waves of heat our tide of talk
did ebb and flow. Our plans were born and grew
like vines that climb tree trunks to reach the sun.

Your jade urn sits beside the fireplace
where like a homing pigeon I return.
I push my back against soft leather, lift
my cold bare feet and plunge them in teal fleece.
I turn and touch the cool lid, say your name.
I sip my tea, feel warmth upon my lips.

Morning Routine

I awaken to black-out blinds' darkness,
wonder how late it is, what day it is.
There is nowhere I have to be, not anymore,
but I get up. I pull on my robe, move through
the house, slide back the heavy glass,
feel the air. I measure out one
tablespoon of medicine, chase
it with whatever's left in the glass,
put a cup of water in the microwave,
check email. Responding like one of Pavlov's
dogs to the beep, I rise, put in one bag of decaf
vanilla chai, watch the fake sugar dissolve.
I take my tea to the living room, set it beside
my chair, place my hands on your jade urn,
touch you the only way I can.

Beyond Reach

"I have to have my husband lift
it from the back to take it off,"
the clerk says when I ask
her how to extricate myself
from the sports bra. I don't tell her
I'm a recent widow.
I just nod as she goes on
to say that I can use a coat hanger if
no one is around.

Later when I step into the shower,
I turn my face away from the faucet,
fold myself into my arms, my forehead
rests against the stall wall. The hot
water runs down my back, tries to drown
the itch that I can't reach, that itch
you can't scratch for me anymore.

No One Visits

Not the living, nor the dead.
I read about how the dead
appear to comfort survivors.
But I've not seen them--not my brother,
my mother, my father. Not you.
I never hear your voice
telling me you're okay, that I will be too.
During happy hour, you don't show up
on the deck to clink your ice cubes
and I don't refresh your Scotch. When I get lost
driving in this city that was supposed to be ours
to explore together, you don't sit
in the passenger seat, tell me where to turn.
And where are you
when the Canucks are about to blow
another Stanley Cup playoff? I could use
your explanation of icing one more time.
I scoffed at those who told me to open
the window so your soul could escape,
but I slid back the glass, shook my head
at those who suggested you might need
my permission to die, but I whispered
it was okay for you to end your suffering.
My grief trumps my disbelief so I talk to you,
try to reach you by touching your urn, and against
all rational thought, I wonder if you are floating
in the ether, waiting for me to believe
just long enough to let you come calling.

Left Unsaid

I want to know
what your eyes saw,
your chameleon eyes,
as hazel, green, and blue
emptied to gray.
Did you see me there
at your bedside?
Could you feel my love
when I laid a hand
on your chest to ride
out its final movement?
When you opened
your mouth at the end,
what was it you
wanted to say?

What We'd Say

If our old Shanghai friends
should visit, our shared
memories would bring to life
the Mock Rock wedding
when you bewigged
and kohl-eyed, swinging
a multi-colored stuffed
Ikea snake, lip synced
Alice Cooper's "School's Out
for Summer". We'd resurrect
your rendition of Gaston
in *Picasso at the Lapin Agile,*
using your Montreal gas
station French to utter
with perfection the line:
I've got to pee.

They'd make mention of my
favorite picture of you
that sits on the coffee table,
the one of you standing
on The Great Wall. We'd
relive the early November
snow chilling the Beijing air
clean. We'd talk about Tibet
and marvel at the irony of me
getting so sick at Everest
Base Camp that spring while
you stood stalwart capturing
people and mountains
with your camera.

And just before they'd leave,
while standing at the door,
we'd shake our heads,
remark on your last
performance five years later
as the butler who did it
in a murder mystery, your
memory starting to flicker,
the cast nobly improvising
when you flubbed your lines,
a portent of things to come.

Love Locks

We climbed Huangshan, half-hidden in
its shroud of clouds, looking just the way
Qing Dynasty artists depicted mountains,
wielding dry brushes to paint broad strokes,
those stone peaks rising up out of white
foam oceans to pierce a flint sky.

Inside the mist, hung an endless chain
of brass locks engraved with lovers' names.
We watched couples creep to the edge, toss
over keys to their lock. We brought no lock,
threw no keys, hadn't known about this
chance to make our bond unbreakable
with one long climb, one simple toss.

Swamped

I've read about the five stages of grief,
how they aren't linear, but come in waves,
so that just when I have my feet under
me again, I am slammed broadside, a wall
of sorrow brought on by the perfect storm:
me telling the story of how we met
at Sloppy Joe's bar to a well-meaning
friend, hearing our song on the radio,
Red Red Wine, not Neil's but the reggae one
we danced to at our wedding, then finding
your brass nameplate in my desk, its luster
dulled. I close my eyes, trace the J, and feel
its curve on my skin, hard and cold, like your
lips when I kissed them for the last time.

Phenomenon

I found a dead bat
in the basement. I left
it right there on the concrete
floor. I didn't touch it, just studied
it. I'd never seen a bat up close,
its spindly limbs, its folded wings,
its origami shape. And then today,
there was a small bird laid out
on the driveway, eyes open like yours
were when you died and I began
to wonder if lots of things would show up
dead now, like when you buy a new car
and as you drive it home, you see
that same model everywhere you look.

The Nature of Things

In my latest dream
of you, vultures tear
at your body, feast on
your flesh, not to be
vicious, but to survive.

I'm not that different
from them as I clutch
at your memory, savor
bits of you, not to be
morbid, but to endure.

Three Chairs, Three Glasses

Now when I
entertain,
they sit beside your jade
urn, avoid your name,
talk around you,
only safe topics,
how hot it is,
friends
in Shanghai,
their new
jobs, fear
of tears, keep
things light,
keep
to the light, stay
light,
laugh.

Knowing When

Three-day hangovers told me
to quit staying out all night drinking,
aching feet told me to give away
my three-inch heels, dimpled thighs
and flabby arms told me to start
wearing Bermuda shorts and short
sleeves, a wrinkled brow announced
the time for bangs. The IRS has rules
for when widows file separate returns,
but how long after your death do I stop
calling myself Mrs.? When will I stop
saying we? When do I start wearing
my wedding ring on the right hand? Or
should I bury it with yours? Two gold
circles in the wooden box on my dresser.

Survival

Like a creature
in mid-flight,
the blur of wings,
the hum of activity,
I must keep moving.

I fight the urge
to still my limbs,
to separate from
the swarm, for
to land is to die.

Today is Thanksgiving

I'm preparing the dish I'll take to share
with others. Families will be there,
and couples. I hope they realize how lucky
they are to have one another. I start to feel
sad, sorry for myself really, because I'm alone,
but then I think about my life, what it was,
what I have now. And I know, I wouldn't trade
what we had for anything. Not even the years
of watching you decline as you struggled to walk,
to talk, to eat, as you tried to remember people
you'd always known. I loved the road trips
we used to take. That time we took the back roads
through Georgia stopping at roadside stands to buy
Vidalia onions and those juicy peaches. Or the time
we drove from Key West to Montreal, camping
in the rustic section in West Virginia. We laughed
because what part of West Virginia isn't rustic?
We looked forward to the caramel apple pie at Denny's
and Snickers, necessities to keep us driving. We'd listen
to audio books and NPR as we racked up
the miles in our Ford truck. Sometimes Chester
would wriggle himself through the camper window
to join us in the front seat, his 100 pound body
on my lap, his tongue hanging out of his mouth,
his ears swept back by the wind. I was the navigator,
learning to read a map, guessing about exits and turns
to make. We couldn't know then, that later,
I'd be the one making all of the decisions. You were
the one who decided what house to buy, what car,
which puppy to take home and then at the job fair,
you said, "Let's go to Shanghai." And I said yes,

because I would go anywhere with you. You gave me
the heat of the tropics and the energy of huge Asian cities.
We journeyed to deserts and mountains, oceans and forests.

Today is Thanksgiving and I miss you,
and your appetite for turkey. Today is Thanksgiving,
and I am grateful for every year of the life we had together

Broken

As I open the cabinet,
a jar of black sesame seeds
tumbles out and chips
the lip of your Life is Good
mug I've used to drink my tea
ever since you got too sick
to use it six years ago. I'd fill
it with hot water and a tea bag,
let it steep. I'd read the words,
and think of that summer you
took a writing class in Kuala Lumpur,
where each morning you walked
to the shop around the corner
from your hotel and drank coffee
as you wrote in your journal. You
liked that mug so much, you bought
one to bring home. You were trying
hard to be happy then, trying to shake
off the cynicism that was your nature.
Seeing these words was a reminder
to enjoy each day, as if you knew then,
how little time was left.

You Were The Photographer

For a long time, it was me in the pictures: tarring the roof
of the trailer, kissing the dog, windblown at the back of the boat.

There's the shot of us drinking beer at the picnic sponsored
by the hospital where you worked when we first met. Of course

we have the wedding pictures, me with your soccer team, you
with your niece and her violin, the standard ones with the judge

and the cake. After you learned to set the timer, there were less
of me and more of us: our one year wedding anniversary

in fancy clothes on our way to dinner. I always laugh at our first
Christmas in Shanghai photo, around that tiny tree, wearing

our gifts, you in Rudolph underwear, me in a cashmere sweater.
Then I got my own camera and started shooting photos of you:

in your Jeep, with the dog in the MG, sailing with your mother,
    beside
the Greek god fireplace in that funky Italian restaurant on your
    birthday,

hiking The Great Wall of China, you surrounded by rice paddies in
    Bali,
drinking a scotch on the back deck in that Aussie hat I bought you,

your arm around your nephew at his jazz performance, eating corn
on the cob with old friends in our treetop house. And then when you

got sick, I became the sole photographer. I took pictures of you lying
in bed or in the sling, there's the one with our heads together smiling,

joking with Santa Claus in the nursing home, me standing behind your wheelchair, both of us in sun hats at the park.

Moments in frames, encased in magnetic sleeves, captured on computer screens, so that now, everywhere I look, I see your face.

Now

Ever since I fell onto the broken
sidewalk bruising my chin
like a plum, tearing open
my hand in such a way
it had to be sewn shut,
I don't bounce my way
to work anymore, don't
revel in the sunshine,
don't daydream. Now
I'm careful to step around
the ruts and cracks.

Will any future love
be like that, cautious
and guarded, now
that I've taken the fall
from delirium to devotion
to despair, now that my heart's
been bruised, its edges left
ragged by your death?

Robert Frost said, "Poetry is when an emotion has found its thought and the thought has found words." "That's why I've tried to do with my grief: find the words that share the thoughts," says **Karen Moulton**, widow, international teacher, and poet. Moulton started writing for her local newspaper in high school and minored in journalism at West Virginia University. In more recent years, she has completed courses from Stanford University's Online Writer's Studio and participated in several online poetry workshops led by Kim Addonizio. Finishing Line Press published her first chapbook, *One Year Ago Today and Other Poems of Revelation*, in 2011.

In this second collection by Moulton, we learn what life was like following her husband's death, especially that first summer, when her days were not spent by his side at the nursing home, which had been her routine for the past five years.

Moulton currently teaches in Taipei, Taiwan, and spends summers in her home in Bellingham, Washington.

CPSIA information can be obtained at www.ICGtesting.com
Printed in the USA
LVOW10s0712210616

493412LV00008B/57/P